kittens

understanding and
caring for your pet

Written by

Claire Horton-Bussey

kittens

understanding and
caring for your pet

Written by
Claire Horton-Bussey

magnet®
steel

Magnet & Steel Publishing

www.magnetandsteelpublishing.com

ISBN: 978-1-907337-12-3
ISBN: 1-907337-12-1

Contents

Foreword

Kittens are fantastic fun – playful, comical, loving and energetic; it's easy to spend hours just watching them, playing with them, petting them and enjoying them to the full. But they don't stay kittens, of course – though many remain young at heart throughout their lives.

The very best news is that kittens grow up to be cats, which are just as beautiful and, in many ways, better companions. Adult cats spend longer in one place – particularly laps – than erratic little kits that race hither and thither, pouncing on anything that moves and scaling your curtains or trouser legs for fun, hell-bent on seeing how many of their nine lives they can use up!

The great advantage of homing a kitten rather than an adult cat is that you can mould him to your home and family, socialising him thoroughly to ensure he is confident around children, dogs, other cats and so on.

You don't have this luxury with an adult cat, and have to hope that someone else has already done the hard work for you.

Compared with some pets, kittens are simple to care for. They don't need expensive, specialist equipment, as some reptiles do, and they don't need taking for a walk, like a dog. But just because they are independent creatures, it doesn't mean they are entirely self-sufficient: a kitten will need you to play with him, train him, groom him, and simply stroke and enjoy his company.

As well as the time commitment, it is also important to ensure that you can afford the life-long responsibility that cat ownership entails, including food and vet bills, and also that everyone in the household is in agreement about sharing the home with a feline.

This book will help you all understand how to raise and care for a kitten throughout his life, ensuring he is happy and healthy – and a joy to share your home with.

Introduction

Cats are one of the most popular pets in the world, outnumbering dogs in Britain and America. There are an estimated 8.6 million pet cats in the UK and a staggering 60 million in the United States. More than 90 per cent of these are non-pedigree cats, affectionately known as moggies.

According to the Pet Food Manufacturers' Association, people opt for a cat as a pet for companionship and love, and because they are easy to care for and get along with other species.

Cats and kittens are very adaptable and can be found in all sorts of households – single homes, busy families, older couples, country or town, flat or mansion. Provided they are safe from roads and other dangers and can have their basic care needs met, a kitten will thrive in many different living environments.

Unlike dogs, cats can be left for hours while their owners work, though it's advisable to spend at least a few days with a new kitten, to settle him in and supervise him. In addition, cats are small and do not require a large home or garden. Indeed, some are kept successfully as indoor house cats in places where road-traffic is too hazardous, provided they are given adequate opportunities to express their natural behaviours (hunting, climbing, scratching etc.) indoors.

Their size also ensures that kittens and cats can be picked up and carried easily – it's far easier taking a cat to the vet than a reluctant St Bernard dog, for example – they don't require masses of food, and they fit on a lap perfectly well for a cuddle!

Kittens come in many colours and patterns, and, for those who would like even further choice, there are many pedigree breeds to choose from. There really is a kitten for almost every taste!

Taming the wildcat

Watch a cat playing in the garden or stalking a toy on the hearthrug and it's not difficult to see where his origins lie. He may have been domesticated for several thousand years, but he still retains many features of his wild ancestor, the African wildcat (Felis sylvestrus libyaca).

The cat family (Felidae) is a varied group, and, in common with all carnivorous mammals, is thought to have descended from miacids, developed around 60 million years ago. By around 100,000 years ago, the cat family had developed into Panthera (lions, tigers and other big cats), Acinonyx (cheetahs, who are unable to retract their claws), and Felis (smaller wildcats, such as lynx and the African wildcat).

The domesticated cat's story began with the agricultural revolution of the Neolithic Stone Age when humans began storing their crops, but rats and mice posed a serious threat to the reserves – and hence people's lives. Fortunately, cats were equally as attracted to the granaries – not for the grain but for the easy rodent pickings! People welcomed the cats' help in eradicating the rodents, and, over time, the cats became less fearful of humans and more relaxed around the human settlements, which, as well as offering an easy source of food, also offered protection from wild predators that were fearful of humans.

With a combination of some kind of genetic mutation occurring, together with selective breeding (people-tolerant cats in the settlement mating with others of a similar character), the cat became domesticated over time – although he's more than capable of reverting to the wild and surviving by his own wits if necessary.

His fortunes have waxed and waned through the ages, from being worshipped in Ancient Egypt to being persecuted in the Middle Ages for being thought of as the witch's familiar, but he is now securely top of our list of favourite pets – a spot he's unlikely to relinquish any time soon.

How many?

|How many?

It's often said that cats are solitary creatures, but this isn't strictly true. Yes, cats are lone hunters, unlike some animals that hunt in pairs or packs, but they can live happily in groups. This is evident from watching feral cat groups, where close, lasting relationships can be seen, particularly in the adult females, who help to nurse and raise kittens together.

An only cat in a home will be more than content, provided his needs are met, but many cats can – and do – live happily with one or more of their own kind, particularly when young. Two kittens are likely to play with each other and bond closely, whereas an older puss may be less tolerant of having his tail stalked and pounced on! The key to success is to ensure both kittens are sociable and friendly (that they each receive plenty of petting, lap-warming, play and quiet time alone, when they can escape to a snooze spot away from others if they want to).

Most squabbles arise over competition for resources. So ensure that each feline in the home has a litter tray, bed, food and water bowl, and 'high point' (somewhere such as a high windowsill). And remember: you also count as a resource, so make sure you give your lap and attention to each puss, too!

Personality also plays a part, of course. Some cats are simply loners and only you will know if your cat would accept a newcomer. Perhaps you have an oldie that has never shared his home with a feline friend and is aggressive to any cat that strays into his garden, or maybe you have a younger, very territorial cat or one that is very nervous and fearful. However, such cats are generally in the minority. Most will accept a new kitten in the home provided the situation is handled carefully (see page 72).

With time, they will become increasingly confident around each other, and, in many cases, will be curling up next to each other for a nap before you know it!

Which breed?

Cats do not have the same diversity as dog breeds – they are fairly uniform in size and appearance – unlike, say, a Chihuahua and an Irish Wolfhound. But there are distinct breeds with their own distinct looks and personalities. Here are some of the most popular.

Bengal

Created by a geneticist, Jean Mill, keen to conserve the wild Asian Leopard Cat, the Bengal's popularity lies in how similar it looks to small wildcats.

Large, muscular and with an awesome patterned coat (spotted or marbled tabby in brown, white or silver), the Bengal may look wild, but breeders have worked hard to ensure that early aggression and fear problems have been removed. Nowadays, the Bengal is a friendly, gentle cat, playful and energetic, and a loving addition to the family home.

British
Shorthair

From selectively breeding ordinary domestic cats, breeders fixed the British Shorthair type in the early 1800s.

The breed was close to extinction by the Second World War, so Persian and Oriental blood was introduced. With his round face, large eyes and thick coat, this is an attractive puss, whose coat comes in many colours and patterns, including white, cream, blue, lilac, black and chocolate, with bi-colour, tortoiseshell, spotted and tabby variations. Playful and loving, he has a strong, cobby, muscular body and is renowned as a great hunter.

Burmese

The breed was created by breeding a Sealpoint Siamese from Thailand to a female cat that was taken to America from Rangoon, the Burmese capital, in 1930.

Careful subsequent breeding established the breed type, though two types have since emerged: the European Burmese (which is more Oriental in appearance, with a slender, athletic body, longer legs and a more refined face) and the American (which has a shorter nose and rounder skull). Both types have the short, velvety coat, which comes in various colours with tortoiseshell variations. Vocal, clever and playful, the Burmese loves human company, with tortoiseshell said to be more extrovert than other coat types.

|Manx

As her name suggests, the Manx cat comes from the Isle of Man, off the north west coast of Britain. He is most famous for his short or non-existent tail.

Legend has it that Noah shut the door on the cat's tail when he closed the Ark, but in fact the breed's tail is due to a genetic mutation that occurred naturally at least 300 years ago and was bred on into future generations due to the limited gene pool on the island. Manx cats can be any colour and pattern and any coat length. A long-haired Manx is also known as a Cymric.

Siamese

One of the oldest pedigree breeds of domestic cat, dating back to around 1300, the Siamese once roamed the palaces of Siam, as he was considered a treasure of the royalty.

Taking the cats out of the country was a sin punishable by death. Fortunately, they did eventually make their way out of what is now Thailand, and have been a firm favourite with cat lovers the world over ever since. This is hardly surprising, given their majestic good looks and incredible characters. The show-type Siamese has become very exaggerated in recent decades, but the traditional Siamese type continues to be bred by those who are not such fans of the extreme look of the modern breed. Vocal, active, loving, demanding and strong-willed, the Siamese is highly intelligent. This cat needs an owner who will give lots of attention, play and love.

Persian

Like the Siamese, the Persian has also changed dramatically due to the show world and changing tastes. The modern Persian has a much flatter, squashed-in face, a longer, more luxurious coat, and a larger head than its forbears.

Traditional, more moderate-looking Persians can still be found, however, for those that are not keen on the exaggerated type. Regardless of type, grooming is a big part of owning this breed; the coat (which comes in a plethora of colours and patterns) is thick and long and needs daily brushing. It is just as well, then, that the Persian is so laid-back and enjoys the attention of being pampered. Generally a calm cat, the Persian isn't as energetic as some breeds and loves to snooze on a lap or in a warm bed.

Moggie

A moggie is a mixed breed/non-pedigree cat. Benefiting from 'hybrid vigour', moggies are generally healthier than pedigree cats, which have a closed gene pool and are therefore more prone to breed-related health disorders.

Moggies are cheaper to purchase than pedigrees, come in a coat type and colour to suit every taste, and are easier to obtain than many purebreds. There may be long waiting lists for pedigree kittens, and even longer distances to a suitable breeder.

Sourcing
your kitten

The best place to find a kitten is from a reputable rescue centre. Here you will find a good selection of cats of all ages – perhaps even a pedigree – who will have been vet-checked and handled and assessed by experienced staff. This is preferable to buying a kitten from a private advert in a newspaper or from the internet, where you may not be certain of the animal's health and history, and where the vendors may not offer the same post-sales advice and support.

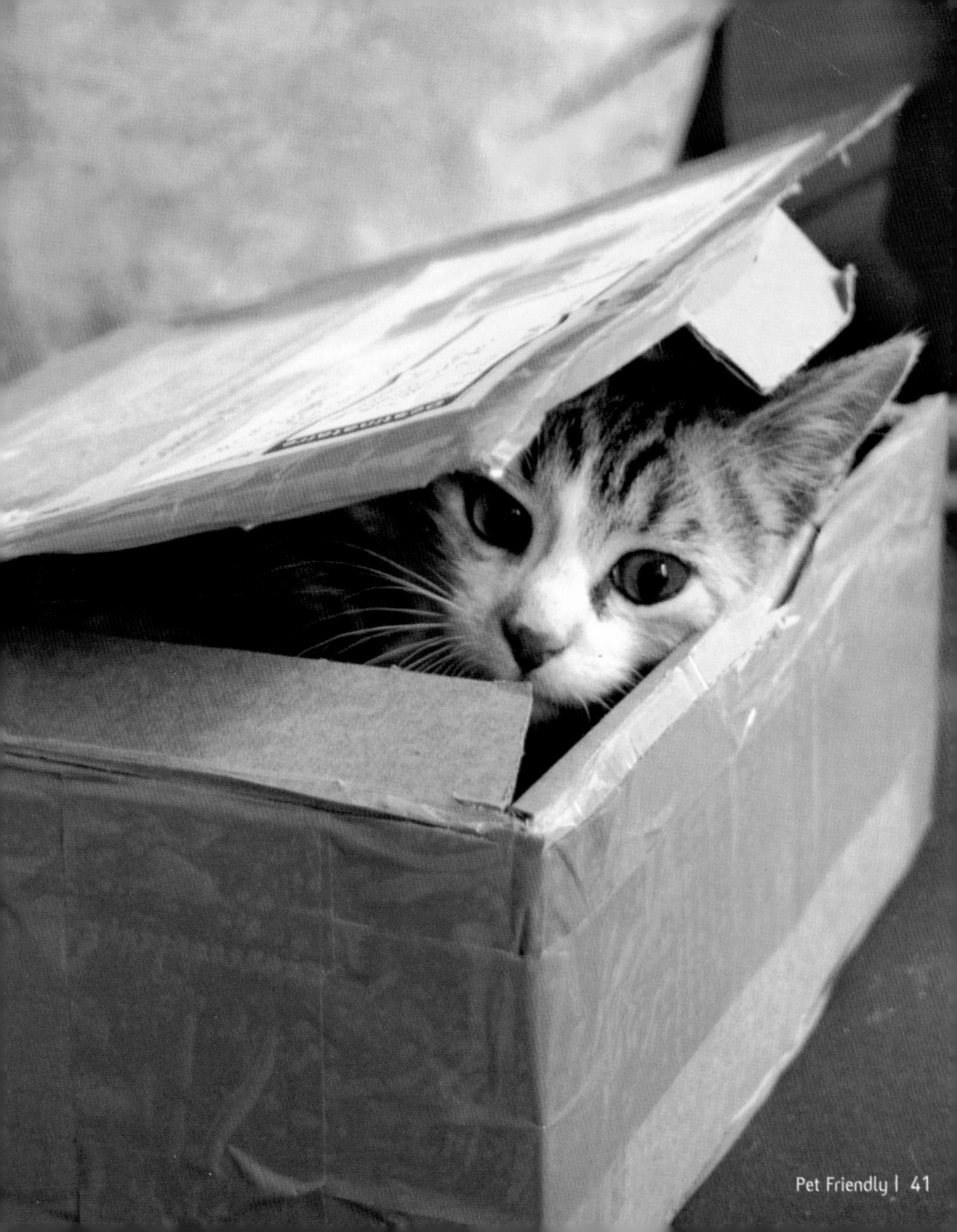

There are many types of rehoming organisations. Some rehome dogs and cats (and sometimes rabbits and other small pets, too), some just specialise in cats, and some are dedicated to just one breed, such as the Siamese.

If you want a rescue kitten of a particular breed, you may have to wait quite some time for the right cat to become available, especially in the numerically small breeds, but if you would like a moggie, then you will be spoilt for choice. Rescue centres are usually heaving with beautiful cats and kittens of every description. Some may be there because they have strayed and cannot be reunited with their owners, but most kittens will have either been born in rescue (with mum having been handed in or found as a stray), or found dumped. Some are handed in as people have had a litter and are unable to find them homes.

Every rescue centre has its own policies, but you will generally be interviewed, to assess your family and home's suitability and to find out your wants and needs. A home-check will also be performed.

Sexing your kitten

Sexing your kitten

Identifying the sex of a kitten can be a tricky business. Hopefully the breeder/ rescue centre will have accurately determined if you have a boy or a girl kitten, but it's as well to check! Even vets get it wrong sometimes – particularly if the youngster is just a few weeks old. It becomes more obvious as the kitten grows, and by the time the kitten is old enough to be rehomed, there should be no doubt whether you'll need a blue collar or a pink one!

The best way to remember it is to think in terms of punctuation! From behind, with the cat's tail up, the female cat's bottom and genitals will look like an upside-down exclamation mark.

A male cat will look more like a colon (i.e. one small circle above another). Also, the gap between the anus and the genitals is shorter in the female than in the male. You might even see a slight swelling just below the anus in a male cat - these are the testicles.

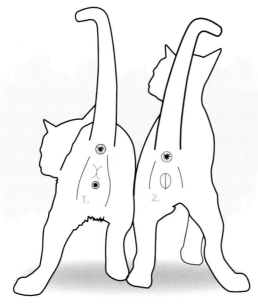

male (tomcat)	female (queen)
1. penile opening (circle)	2. vulva (vertical slit)

Preparing your home

Before bringing your kitten home, it's important that you prepare a room that puss can call his own. A small box room or spare bedroom is ideal. Cats, when stressed, seek small hiding places where they can feel safe and protected. Introducing a kitten to your entire home and expecting him to settle in straight away is asking too much. First, get him used to his special 'cat room' and then, as he grows in confidence, he will venture out and start exploring the rest of the house in his own time, returning to his safe 'den' if spooked.

Place his bed, litter tray, and food and water bowls in the room, ensuring that the litter tray is as far away from the bed and bowls as it can be.

Put some toys in the room for him to play with (or for you to play with together when you visit the room), and also put a scratching post inside. Make sure the windows are locked (some smart cats can open windows!) and ensure the room is cat-safe (no toxic houseplants, such as Poinsettia or lilies; no irreplaceable heirlooms on a mantelpiece or shelf within the cat's reach, etc).

Next, kitten-proof the rest of the house and garden. Assess each room from a cat's perspective, getting down on your hands and knees if necessary! Don't underestimate the devastation that a kitten can cause in play – whether chasing his own tail, hunting a fly or testing out how high he can scale your curtains. Put breakable ornaments away or display them in a glass cabinet.

Electrical cables are another hazard. Kittens seem genetically programmed to find dangling wires to play with and chew, so gather up excess electrical wire and fasten with a cable tie.

You should also discuss with all family members some basic rules to ensure the new kitten's safety:

- The toilet seat should always be put down when not in use, so a curious puss can't jump in and/or drink from the bowl and ingest any harmful cleaning chemicals.

- Windows should be shut/locked and doors kept closed until your kitten is allowed to go outside – and thereafter, all upstairs windows should be securely closed in case your kitten jumps out. Screens can be fitted to windows that allow air to enter, but prevent a kitten escaping.

- The washing machine and tumble-dryer doors should be kept shut when not in use and the insides should be checked before they are switched on in case your kitten has crept inside. All chemicals and medicines should be shut away (antifreeze, aspirin and paracetemol, for example, can be deadly to cats).

- The shed/garage should always be checked before being locked up, in case your kitten has sneaked inside.

Only use products that are entirely cat-safe in your garden. If you have a pool or pond, these should be covered and ramps should be fitted so that puss can climb out if he falls in.

As part of your preparations, you should also fit a catflap to the back door (unless you want to be pestered relentlessly to let the cat out and in and out again) and set it to the locked position so your new kitten can't yet escape into the big, wide world.

If you have a dog in the home, fit a stair-gate so your kitten can have the upstairs to himself, away from any canine attention. (If you live in a flat, use a stairgate to shut off a part of your accommodation – perhaps across a corridor to the bedrooms, for example). In time, and with careful introductions, he will be happy to slip through the gate to commune downstairs, but in the early days, he will want to find his feet and settle in, unbothered by the family dog.

Essential
equipment

Essential equipment

A kitten's needs are pretty basic compared with most pets, but there are some essential things you should buy before bringing him home.

Bed

There is a bed to suit every taste and budget. Although you can get ornate four-posters and chaise longues for cats (yes, really!), most have humbler tastes, preferring a pile of freshly laundered washing! A simple, fleecy pad-type bed is a good starting point, or, better still, a hooded cat bed, which will help to make puss feel safe and protected. Place the bed in a corner of the room, or, if it is deep enough, on a windowsill.

Bowls

You will need at least two bowls – one for food and one for water – though four are ideal, so you can wash one set while another set is being used. Choose from plastic, ceramic or stainless steel. In the long-term, the last two are better options, as plastic bowls can scratch eventually and become quite abrasive.

The design is important: cats prefer to eat from shallow bowls rather than deep ones.

Food

Find out in advance what the kitten is fed, so you can get a supply before you bring him home.

Litter accessories

Your kitten should not be allowed outside until he's at least six months old, so you will need a litter tray, scoop, poo bags/nappy sacs (for depositing the poop), cat-safe disinfectant for cleaning, and a supply of cat litter. Even when he is allowed to go outside, you'll still need a tray for night-time use. Cats shouldn't be allowed out after dusk and before dawn for their own safety (they are most at danger of road accidents when it's dark).

If you already have a cat, do still get another tray for the newcomer, as it is recommended that there is one tray per cat. For indoor house cats, who don't go outside, add another extra tray still – so two cats will need three trays between them.

A covered tray, whether with an open front or a cat-flap front, will help to control odours. Some even have filters in the top of the tray. Some kittens prefer the privacy that a covered tray offers, while others can feel claustrophobic and prefer a standard 'open' tray. Do bear in mind that the best way of keeping a sweet-smelling home is to scoop regularly and to change the entire litter regularly – whether the tray has a cover or not. If the litter is very dirty, most cats won't use it and will find a clean corner of the house to relieve themselves instead!

There are many types of litter – wood-based pellets, paper, clay, silica crystals, lightweight, and the type that forms a scoopable clump when it comes into contact with water. Find out what your kitten is used to and get a supply before bringing him home. If you want to change the type of litter, add a little of the new material to the one he's used to already, mix it in, and gradually, over the course of a few days, increase the amount of new to old until a complete change-over has been achieved.

Tip: If your kitten is fussy about the type of litter he uses, try a fine grain, which many cats prefer.

Identification

Most rescue centres will microchip the animals in their care before they are rehomed, but if you get your kitten from another source, then you may have to arrange for your vet to do it. It is a simple procedure where a small chip, the size of a long grain of rice, is inserted under the skin at the back of the neck, between the shoulder blades. This chip contains a unique number, which will be held on a database with your details. If your kitten becomes lost and is scanned by a reader, you can quickly be reunited. Occasionally, chips fail or migrate, so it is worth asking your vet to scan your cat at her annual check-up, to ensure it's still working properly, but the failure rate is very low and chipping has proved to be a very easy, reliable form of identification.

In addition, a collar and tag is useful so your kitten can be returned to you without a scanner and if it is made of reflective material, it could help improve your kitten's visibility in low light.

It is very important that the collar is a safe one and will not strangle your kitten if it is caught on a branch or something similar. A safety-clip collar that snaps open under pressure is a good option.

Scratching post

Scratching is an important part of feline behaviour. Expecting a kitten not to scratch is entirely unreasonable, but scratching needn't be a problem – as long as you provide him with suitable places to scratch. If he has a scratching post in your lounge, placed at the right height and in the right position, then he'll have no need to put his claws anywhere near your new sofa. Two or three posts should be sufficient for most homes, but you may need more if you have more than one cat, especially if they don't go outside very much.

Avoid carpet-covered scratching boards and posts – your kitten might associate the material with the action and then begin scratching your floor-coverings. Sisal is therefore preferable.

Toys

A good selection of toys is vital. If you spend time regularly playing with your kitten, you will not only strengthen your relationship, but you'll also be helping to keep him active and stimulated (if bored, he will seek amusement by climbing your curtains, 'hunting' your shoelaces etc). Plus, playing with a kitten is simply great fun and a fabulous way of de-stressing!

The range of toys available these days is astonishing, with everything from fishing-rod type toys and balls with bells to remote-controlled mice and multi-toy activity centres. There is something to suit every puss – and purse!

Whatever toys you buy, don't make every one constantly available to your kitten. To keep his interest in them, put them away, and bring out a couple every day for him to play with. The next day, swap them with different toys. Rotating his toys will help to retain their novelty value for longer.

Also remember that toys don't play themselves. Giving him a toy mouse might amuse him for a few minutes, but he'll soon lose interest if it's not wiggled to attract his attention, or thrown for him to chase and 'hunt'.

Feliway

Scent is very important to cats and kittens, not only as a means of communication to other cats but also in terms of his own personal sense of security. If a home smells of his own odour, he will feel far safer than in a new home where there are unfamiliar scents. Kittens put their own smells on objects by rubbing their scent glands against them, particularly facial glands. This is why a kitten will rub his head against the side of furniture, your legs, or against your hand while he is being petted.

Before you bring your new kitten home, put a pheromone diffuser (Feliway) in his room and leave it on continuously for at least four weeks. This will reassure him and really help him to feel secure and 'at home'.

|House Training

House Training

Kittens take to house training remarkably quickly. They are very clean creatures, and, if you give them the right materials in the right places, they will pretty much train themselves! Put a tray of litter in a quiet corner of the house (in the cat room you have prepared for him), show it to him and usually that's it. Job done!

If he does have accidents, then there's a reason why.

Is the tray too close to his bed or food bowls? Understandably, kittens don't like to toilet near where they sleep or eat. Perhaps the litter isn't pleasant for him to walk on (some kittens don't like, for example, the wood-type pellets and prefer a fine-grain litter).

Maybe there's not enough privacy and he doesn't feel secure to go – perhaps because it's too busy and people are coming and going, or he's being stalked by another cat when at his most vulnerable.

So ensure there are plenty of trays dotted around the house in a multi-cat household, and make sure the trays are in quiet corners and not busy thoroughfares.

Is the tray clean? Would you like to use a dirty lavatory? Neither would a cat! If you don't scoop poop promptly and change the entire litter regularly, the kitten will find a cleaner place to relieve himself – such as a quiet spot behind your sofa.

If your kitten suddenly becomes incontinent, or, despite your best efforts, continues to have accidents, you must get him seen by a vet, as perhaps there is an underlying health issue, such as a urinary infection that is responsible.

Is your kitten scent-marking rather than toileting? See page 118 for health issues.

If your kitten does have an accident, it is vital that the area is cleaned thoroughly, as he will otherwise be attracted back to the area to repeat his performance! Even if the area smells clean to you, the kitten's sensitive nose will pick up any trace of scent and, if you have used an ordinary household cleaner, the chances are it will contain ammonia or chloride, which are also found in urine and can tempt a cat back to the area!

Use a proprietary cleaner or a warm solution of biological washing powder (10 per cent) to wash the area, and then wipe with water and dry. Finally, go over lightly with an alcohol wipe or spray a fine mist of surgical spirit over, though this is not recommended for fabric surfaces. Of course, you should do this cleaning routine on a small, unnoticeable part of the surface first, to check that it is safe to continue.

If your kitten returns to the area out of habit, then move the furniture around so he can't get to the same spot again.

Note: Always wear gloves to change litter and to clean out the litter tray. Pregnant women and those with compromised immune systems should avoid handling litter because of the small risk of Toxoplasmosis, a parasitic disease which can be passed on via animal faeces.

Family introductions

Family introductions

Introducing a kitten to an existing cat is often much smoother than with another adult cat, as the youngster is sexually immature and therefore not considered a threat. It's worth considering a kitten of the opposite sex to the cat you already have, to help reduce any rivalry issues. It goes without saying that the cats should be neutered.

Same-sex cats can get on well, too, of course, depending on their personalities, how they are introduced, and providing you ensure that each kitten/cat has enough space and access to important resources (bed, food, litter tray, and you!).

Give your new kitten a cat-safe room. Get him settled in this room, door shut initially, so he doesn't venture out – and your existing cat doesn't venture in!

Get the cat and kitten used to each other's scent before they even meet. Smell is very important to cats and it is helpful if they are familiar with each other's scent before meeting in the flesh.

Stroke one cat, paying particular attention to the cheeks/sides of the mouth, and then go and stroke the other cat. Swapping their blankets/beds is another way of intermingling their scents, as is moving the new kitten out of his room for a short time while the resident cat explores his den.

For a face-to-face meeting, it's important that first impressions are good ones – and that there is no chance of the two fighting or chasing/fleeing. Using a puppy training crate is one option. Put the kitten's bed and litter tray inside, cover the top of the crate with a blanket, so it's cosy and den-like, and then let the resident cat investigate. The cats will be able to see and interact with each other – safely. A Feliway diffuser in the room may help to promote calmness.

If you don't have access to a crate, a cat-carrier can be used for short, supervised introductions, but the kitten shouldn't be left inside for prolonged periods.

If the cats ignore each other, great! If there is any signs of aggression, distract them and then reward any calm behaviour with some tasty chicken or a similar treat. Feed the cats in the same room.

Time the first few 'free' meetings to occur before a meal, so both cats are hungry and likely to concentrate on their meals, not each other. Do ensure there is plenty of space between them – feeding them in opposite sides of the room and ideally in high-up locations, such as on a table/windowsill/cupboard, so they feel safe.

After a few of these introductions, the novelty of the other will probably wear off and you can let them loose in the house to choose where they spend their time and how they interact.

Canine chums

Only you will know if your dog is cat-friendly. If he gets very excitable when he sees cats in the garden, then you must get him properly assessed by a behaviourist before even thinking about introducing a kitten to your home. Terriers and sighthounds have a particularly high prey-drive – after all, they were bred for generations to hunt small, furry, fast-moving animals – and although many can live happily with cats, extra-special care should be taken to ensure they are well-socialised to cats and are introduced and supervised closely.

Install a stair-gate so that puss can come downstairs if he chooses to, but the dog cannot hassle him. His 'cat-safe' room should be upstairs, so he feels completely secure, knowing the dog cannot gain access.

Once puss is settled in his room and feels secure and confident, then think about introducing him to the dog. First, introduce their scent (as above) and swap bedding.

For a face-to-face meeting, it's important that they get their relationship off on a good footing – with no chasing.

If a dog learns that he can make a kitten run, your cat is at risk of forever being viewed as a great toy – whose batteries never run out! So, after the dog has had a walk, keep him on a lead and arrange for a friend or family member to bring your kitten into the room, placing him on a high spot where he feels safe and cannot be reached by the dog. Here he will be able to observe the dog from a distance. Reward the dog if he looks away and ignores your kitten; if he shows interest, distract him calmly.

Short, frequent introductions of this sort will soon get both pets used to the sight of each other and the novelty will wear off.

A training crate can also be used (as for the kitten-to-cat introductions).

When the pets are ready for 'free' meetings, off-lead, ensure that there are plenty of upward escape routes for the kitten, so he doesn't need to dash away at floor level if threatened. Hopping up to a high surface if necessary is preferable, as it doesn't instigate a chase.

Never leave the kitten and dog unsupervised.

If you need help, don't hesitate in contacting a reputable animal behaviourist/trainer. If you get the feline-canine relationship off to a good start, it will save many future years of angst!

Outdoors

Outdoors

Letting your kitten outside for the first time can be a nerve-wracking business. Unlike dogs, cats have their own life when outside and with this freedom comes inevitable danger – from traffic, from curiosity (being shut in other people's houses, sheds or garages when being nosy), from being poisoned due to exposure to other gardeners' pesticides or from eating a mouse or rat that has ingested toxins, or from other animals (not only getting into scraps with other cats but perhaps stray dogs). Other dangers come from being spooked by thunder or fireworks and running, petrified, until the kitten is utterly lost.

This makes the outside world sound a terrifying place – and some people choose to keep indoor house cats only (see page 93). But, in truth, provided you take some basic precautions, the risks are minimised and many cats live to a ripe old age, having lived a full and eventful life.

- Do not let your kitten out until he has been neutered, vaccinated and microchipped.

- Do not let him out unsupervised until he is at least six months old.

- Presumably you don't live near a busy road. If you do, puss will have to be an indoor house cat until you move to a safer area. Letting him outside really will be risking him life.

- Make sure you keep your kitten in from just before dusk until after dawn. Cats are crepuscular (most active at dawn and dusk), and if they are concentrating on hunting, they are less alert to dangers, such as road traffic.

- Put a high-visibility collar on him, to maximize his chances of being seen.

- Make your own garden as enticing as possible. For example, if there's a quiet, safe spot he can snooze, and some trees he can climb or sit in (or an artificial observation spot, such as a DIY activity tree), then he's likely to spend more time in your garden.

Releasing a reckless, foolhardy kitten who seems to think he's invincible can be worrying, but take heart that kittens are usually more robust than they look and instinct quickly kicks in when they are in the great outdoors.

The time that he should be kept indoors varies from individual to individual, with the general consensus being that when they try to get out, they are ready to go out. Certainly, keep your kitten in until he's neutered, vaccinated and microchipped and at least six months old. If you have an older kitten, three weeks is the minimum time he should spend indoors, to give him time to bond with you and to imprint a sense of where his new home is. If he is still timid after this time, wait longer. Some cats need as long as three months; some much less.

Until he is ready to venture outside, ensure all doors and windows are closed and cat-flaps locked, and be careful when opening outside doors that your kitten can't make a run for freedom!

When the day comes to introduce him to the garden, make sure the conditions are right. It should be a fine day (no threat of thunder storms that could spook him), not during firework season, and ideally with children at school (so you can fully focus on the kitten and he isn't distracted by them).

- Prepare something really yummy, some diced chicken, for example, and ensure he doesn't have any breakfast before you let him outside.

- Open the back door and walk outside, calling him to you and showing him the diced chicken. Give him a treat when he comes to you and make a fuss of him.

- Let him sniff around and explore the garden, and call him to you every few minutes, giving him some tasty chicken when he obeys.

- After about 10 minutes, go inside, call him to you, give him the remaining chicken and then his meal.

- Short, frequent visits outside are best initially, so he gets used to coming inside and out, while venturing further each trip out. With each visit, you can gradually prolong the time that he's outside.

- Keep the back door open while he's out, so he has a fast, easy way back into the house in case he's spooked. Once you are confident that he knows his way back, then close the door and make sure the cat-flap is unlocked.

Cat-flap

Your kitten might have already encountered a cat flap. Some rescue centres use them to link the indoor/sleeping area of a pen, with an outdoor enclosure. But if your puss hasn't seen one before, he'll probably work it out for himself soon enough – it isn't rocket science, after all! So, before he's allowed to venture outside, keep the flap locked, and, when he is free to come and go, remember to lock it at night, to keep him indoors.

If your cat needs a helping paw, here's how to start from scratch:

First, make sure the cat can easily access the flap. It sounds obvious, but check that it's not too high!

Making sure it's unlocked, sit outside with some high-value treats – diced chicken, for example, with your puss inside, and call him through. If he noses the flap, praise him warmly and show him the treats you have.

If he uses the flap to get to you, reward him with the chicken and then switch positions, with you inside the house and him outside. Call him again and reward when he uses the flap to come inside.

If he doesn't nose the flap, show him the chicken through the flap pane and call him encouragingly.

If he still doesn't attempt to use it, arrange for a family member or friend to sit the other side of the door with the kitten and to push the flap open so he can get to you – and his chicken reward! Once he's had a treat he'll be eager for another, so repeat the exercise, this time with the helper opening the flap slightly less. Repeat, until the kitten can use the flap without help.

House cats

Some people choose to keep their cats permanently indoors, because of the risks to the cat's safety; and some people have no choice – because of the cat's own health and risk to others. For example, if you adopt a kitten with a known health problem, such as FIV or feline leukaemia, he is at risk of passing on the disease to other cats and so will have to remain under your close control. Deaf cats, too, should be kept indoors, for their own safety.

With a house cat, you have to work extra hard to ensure your puss's needs are met within the confines of your home, particularly with an energetic youngster. If he is deprived of opportunities to express his natural behaviour – hunting, climbing, scratching, etc – he will become bored and unhappy, and serious behavioural problems can develop.

Is he sociable? Would he enjoy a feline playmate? If he has a health problem, such as FIV, this may not be possible – unless you get another cat that also has FIV, for example.

Play with him as much as you can throughout the day, using a variety of toys to maintain his interest.

Set aside time for regular training sessions. Kittens are very intelligent and take well to clicker training. Using his brain will keep him mentally alert and stop him stagnating – plus it's fun and strengthens the pet/owner bond.

Kitty Kongs, stuffed with catnip, or puppy Kongs stuffed with pate or cheese, will keep him amused, as will something like the Kong Kickeroo Animal, which promotes wrestling and hind-paw kicking. Visit your pet shop and trawl the internet for the latest products to keep puss busy – mentally and physically.

Indoor grass (from pet shops) is a must for a house cat. Cats enjoy nibbling grass and it's thought to provide essential roughage to prevent constipation and to allow furballs to be brought up.

Consider building (or having built) a pen that he can access from the house – where he can feel the wind in his fur and watch the world go by.

Behaviour

Adfærd

Katte er ligetil, og de lider sjældent af adfærdsforstyrrelser, hvis de har haft en god opvækst, er helt socialiserede, og deres basale behov imødekommes. For en killing er tidlig kontakt og positive, glade oplevelser med mange forskellige mennesker afgørende. Det er også vigtigt, at den tidligt møder forskellige synsindtryk og lyde (for eksempel vaskemaskinen, børn, en venlig hund osv.) Hvis den føler sig tryg og ved, at den hurtigt kan finde et smuthul, vil den lære, at den ikke er i fare.

Hvis der alligevel opstår adfærdsproblemer, handler det i mange tilfælde simpelthen om at forstå, hvorfor killingen opfører sig, som den gør (måske er den destruktiv pga. kedsomhed), og give den det, den mangler (i dette tilfælde en mere varieret og stimulerende leg – og mulighed for at træne krop og sind).

Hvis ikke du er i stand til at løse problemet, må du ikke tøve med at kontakte en ekspert, eftersom adfærdsspørgsmål hurtigt kan blive værre. Jo tidligere, der tages hånd om et problem, jo bedre!

Din dyrlæge vil først tjekke, om der ligger helbredsmæssige årsager til grund for problemet, inden han henviser til en passende ekspert – en, som har kompetencer og erfaring med at regulere katteadfærd på en venlig, ikke-straffende, belønningsbaseret måde.

Mad

Mad

De fleste kattekillinger vil spise hvad som helst, du giver dem. Nogle er dog tilbøjelige til at ændre mening, især hvis deres ejer forkæler dem ved at udskifte deres aldeles udmærkede, om end intetsigende, tørkost med saftig kylling eller tun, i samme øjeblik killingen – af en eller anden grund – ikke er interesseret i at spise op. Det tager ikke lang tid for en snu kat at finde ud af, at hvis den afviser et måltid, så kommer der hurtigt noget bedre på bordet!

Det bedste råd er at blive ved med at give katten den mad, den er vant til – så bed opdrætteren eller katteinternatet om kostdetaljer. Et pludseligt skifte i kosten kan medføre diarré, og dette – sammen med den stress, det medfører at flytte til et nyt hjem og finde sig til rette hos en ny familie – kan belaste dens krop betydeligt. Hvis du ønsker at ændre killingens kost, så vent mindst et par måneder, indtil den er helt på plads, og gør det så hen over en uge til ti dage, hvor du gradvist erstatter kattens sædvanlige mad med den nye slags, indtil det alt sammen er udskiftet.

Typer af kost

Nu om dage er der både typer og smagsvarianter til enhver smag og ethvert budget. Der er endda dyrlæge-kost, der passer til specifikke sundhedsproblematikker. Tørkost er normalt fuldkost – hvilket betyder, at den indeholder alle de næringsstoffer, der er nødvendige for, at katten holder sig sund. Der er ikke brug for at give nogen form for tilskud. Det er godt for en kats tandpleje at knase de hårde "kiks" (modsat dåsemaden, der sætter sig på tænderne), og tørkosten bliver ikke dårlig eller tiltrækker fluer, sådan som dåsemad kan gøre det.

Dåsemad lugter også mere, og den sviner mere, men den er også ofte mere tiltrækkende for katte og anbefales til ældre katte, som måske ikke længere har tænder, der kan knuse tørkosten.

Den er også et godt valg, hvis du er nødt til at lokke katten til at spise, eller hvis katten er i risiko for at få en urinvejssygdom (FLUTD).

Både dåsemad og tørkost fås normalt i forskellige aldersvarianter, der præcist matcher kattens skiftende behov. I killingemad er der masser af energi og proteiner. Når din kat er omkring et år gammel og fuldt udvokset, bør den skifte til en voksenvariant, og derefter – ved 7-års alderen – igen til en seniorkost. Der findes også særlig mad til indekatte og til overvægtige katte.

Madtider

Tørkost kan stilles frem om morgenen og være tilgængelig hele dagen, så katten kan spise af den efter behov. Hæld den mængde op, der anbefales på pakken. Eller du kan dele den daglige mængde i to eller tre portioner, som du stiller frem om morgenen, til frokost og om aftenen. Dette kan være at foretrække, hvis du har et hjem med mange katte, hvor en grådig mis måske dykker ned i de andres skåle, når ikke de overvåges.

Dåsemad bør ikke stå fremme hele dagen, da den vil tiltrække fluer og bliver dårlig. "Dåsemad" i poser er efterhånden blevet populær, og med dem er der frisk mad ved hver servering. Der kan også kommes låg på en åbnet dåse, men nogle gadekryds er så kræsne, at de ikke bryder sig om at spise resten af dåsen ved næste måltid!

Vand

Frisk vand skal altid være tilgængelig – det er særligt vigtigt, hvis killingen kun får tørkost. Nogle katte foretrækker rindende vand – og mange katte ses derfor labbe vand i sig ved vandhanen. Der kan fås drikke-springvand til den slags vandbørn. Kattemælk kan købes i små flasker i supermarkedet og hos dyrehandleren, men lad dig ikke friste til at give komælk til din kat. Den vil sikkert drikke den med glæde, men den vil ikke være i stand til at fordøje laktosen (mælkesukkeret), og det kan meget vel bringe uorden i dens mave.

Græs

Killinger og voksne katte nipper græs, når de er ude, og det er vigtigt også at have noget inden døre, hvis ikke din kat må komme ude. Græsset indeholder nogle fibre, der hjælper katten med at fordøje. Det kan også fungere som et naturligt opkastningsmiddel afhjælpe hårbolde og andre forhindringer. Græsset kan sagtens vokse indenfor i små baljer, som killingen kan græsse af.

Pelspleje

Pelspleje

De fleste katte er korthårede gadekryds, der kræver minimal pelspleje. De er fuldt ud i stand til at pleje sig selv. Deres ru tunger børster gennem pelsen, fordeler naturlige olier i den og fjerner døde hår. Men det betyder ikke, at kattene ikke kan bruge en hjælpende hånd. En gennembørstning en gang om ugen vil afhjælpe, at der samles hårbolde. Det vil også mindske mængden af hår, der efterlades rundt omkring på husets tæpper, tøj og møbler. Og det vil styrke jeres forhold, samtidig med at du har chancen for at tjekke for utøj i pelsen og andre fysiske forandringer, der skal ses nærmere på af en dyrlæge, for eksempel knuder eller skrammer.

Nogle racer har dog brug for mere assistance, det gælder specielt i de tilfælde, hvor mennesker har "blandet sig" i det originale kattedesign. For eksempel er perserens pels nu så lang og tyk, at katten ikke selv er i stand til at holde den i en god stand uden hjælp fra et menneske. En perser bliver til et filtret rod på meget kort tid, hvis den overlades til egne evner.

Når du køber eller adopterer en killing, kan opdrætteren eller katteinternatet give dig udførlige råd om, hvilken pelspleje din killing har brug for – ikke kun nu, men også når den er fuldvoksen og har fået sin voksenpels.

Rutiner

Det er meget vigtigt at vænne killingen til at blive børstet. Hvis den vænner sig til oplevelsen, mens den er ung, bliver livet meget lettere i fremtiden – specielt hvis den er langhåret eller halv-langhåret.

Tilvænningen er ikke vanskelig, hvis du gør det til en del af en almindelig kæletur. Ae killingen over det hele, og begynd så simpelthen – når den spinder og er afslappet – at børste den blidt (opbevar børsten ved din bedste lænestol, så den er inden for rækkevidde!). Børst kun et par minutter, giv den en godbid og kæl så for den med hånden igen.

Later, try a couple more minutes. Keep sessions short and frequent, and very gradually extend them in terms of time and the areas groomed.

When he has his adult coat, use the services of a professional groomer if you don't have the time or expertise. If your cat would be stressed by the car journey or visit to a salon, find a groomer that will visit your home.

Health

Health

Kittens are usually pretty robust, healthy creatures – with accidents being a chief cause of a visit to the vet (broken bones, eating something he shouldn't, etc). Kitten-proofing your home and close supervision will help to minimise such accidents, but it's advisable to be safety-conscious (see page 48) and prepared for emergencies. Kittens really do seem to have nine lives, managing to get into – and out of – all sorts of scrapes, but that's not to say that they are invincible!

Keep the cat-carrier in an easily accessible place (not hidden at the back of the garage under a ton of unused garden furniture or in far recesses of the loft), so you can find it, put the kitten inside and drive to the vet as quickly as possible if he needs urgent medical treatment.

On the fridge door, by the phone, or somewhere else that's visible and immediately obvious, write the number of your vet surgery, and keep a pen and piece of paper close by in case you need to write down the details of the out-of-hours emergency contact.

Seek immediate veterinary advice in all cases.

There are plenty of good first-aid sites on the internet that are worth reading, so you are fully prepared for any future emergencies.

Ill-health

Be alert to signs of ill-health so you can contact your vet at the earliest opportunity. The sooner this intervention comes, the better the chances of recovery.

Signs of ill-health are too numerous to list here, but you should be looking out for any change from your cat's usual condition and normal behaviour. If he's sleepier than usual; drinking or eating more or less; if he's grooming more; if he's grumpy or less tolerant of being petted; all of these signs can suggest that something is wrong. More obvious signs are the physical changes: perhaps there's a change in the type and frequency of his toileting habits; perhaps there's a change to his coat, his eyes and/or nose are runny, or he's scratching himself. Has he lost or put on weight? Does his breath smell? Have any lumps appeared?

All of these signs can be spotted quickly if you spend any amount of time with your kitten, and instinct often kicks in, too. "I can't put my finger on it, but my pet just doesn't seem himself" is commonly heard at vet practices around the country, and, from there, the vet can examine the animal for any leads.

Do not ever be tempted to treat the kitten yourself. Many drugs intended for humans – such as paracetemol – are highly toxic to cats. A visit to the professionals at the first sign of illness often means a condition can be treated quickly – and more affordably.

Pet insurance is worth exploring, as unexpected vet bills can be difficult – particularly if, given veterinary advances, specialist treatment is given or a chronic, long-term condition emerges. Do be aware of the different types of policy when researching insurance, as some policies only give 12 months' cover for each condition.

Neutering

Neutering involves removing the testes in males and the ovaries and uterus in females. Neutering your cat is essential, to avoid unwanted pregnancies and to protect his or her health. When so many perfectly healthy cats and kittens are being destroyed for want of a home, breeding a litter of moggies is unforgivable. Even if you have homes for the anticipated kittens, by producing a litter, you will be condemning to death shelter cats that could have been rehomed instead.

Neutering a cat will also prevent spraying in toms, calling in queens and will stop them acquiring sexually transmitted diseases. Toms often fight when competing for a mate, too, and are then at risk of diseases such as calicivirus, FIV and feline leukaemia, for example. Unneutered cats are at increased risk of road accidents, too, as they roam further in search of a mate and are single-minded in their pursuit – to the detriment of their road-sense.

If your kitten isn't already neutered when you adopt him/her, then it's imperative that he is kept indoors – and away from any entire cats of the opposite sex – until he/she is neutered. Your vet will advise you of the best time, dependent on your specific circumstances, but it is generally done at around six months.

Holidays

Holidays

There are many options available if you need to leave your kitten for any length of time. Unlike dogs, cats are pretty low-maintenance and it's not unusual for a neighbour to happily volunteer to call in, feed him, change the litter tray and give him a cuddle for a week. It's far less stressful for the kitten to be in his home environment.

If the friend/neighbour option isn't possible, you could pay a professional pet-sitter to come in and care for the kitten a couple of times a day, or even to live in your home for the full week if you'd prefer and can afford this luxury. Do make sure you go through a reputable agency and check up on the sitter's references. It's also advisable to meet the person in advance of you going away, to talk through the cat's specific needs and routines, and to ensure you are happy to entrust your home and loved one to them. If you are not 100 per cent content, ask the agency for another sitter.

A third option is a cattery. If a kitten has been used to going to a cattery from a young age, he could well be happy with such an arrangement, though most cats, if given the option, would prefer the comfort of home. Vet the cattery carefully, visiting the premises, talking to the staff and asking lots of questions about their experience, the cats' care arrangements, and so on. Your cat will have to be fully vaccinated to be accepted, so ensure you have the necessary boosters done in good time for them to be effective – and have the right paperwork to show as proof.

Weights & measures

If you prefer your units in pounds and inches, you can use this conversion chart:

Length in inches	Length in cm	Weight in Kg	Weight in lbs
1	2.5	0.5	1.1
2	5.1	0.7	1.5
3	7.6	1	2.2
4	10.2	1.5	3.3
5	12.7	2	4.4
8	20.3	3	6.6
10	25.4	4	8.8
15	38.1	5	11

Measurements rounded to 1 decimal place.